Our Journey

Pathway to Purpose

Navigating the Heart Transplant Process

ANDREA ADAMS

ISBN 979-8-89130-090-3 (paperback)
ISBN 979-8-89130-091-0 (digital)

Christian Faith Publishing
832 Park Avenue
Meadville, PA 16335
www.christianfaithpublishing.com

Printed in the United States of America

CHAPTER 1

The Courage to Live
(Leaving the Comfort Zone)

I thought I knew my husband! He is a great guy who loves his family fiercely. I never would have thought, in a million years, that he would ever suggest moving us away from everything and everyone we know. The destination: Phoenix, Arizona. Why? Because God urged him to.

We were born and raised in Elyria and Lorain, Ohio (about twenty-five miles west of Cleveland). Let's call these sister cities. Both are not large and are interchangeable. When describing where we live to strangers, most residents would say we are from the Elyria-Lorain area. We both hail from large, close-knit families. I am the youngest of six siblings, eight including my parents. He is the youngest boy of eight, ten including his parents. From birth until this point, we have lived our entire lives in a twenty-mile radius. including traveling to work.

You could say we grew up together. We met at church when we were both fifteen years old. We started dating at sixteen, but that did not last long. Instead, we became really good friends when we were seventeen and began to hang out together with friends (Cheryl and Michael) all the time. The four of us spent most weekends together having fun. We graduated from high school in 1987. Keith, my soon-to-be husband, went away to Central State University, and I took a year off to work. Then in 1988, I went away to University of Akron, Keith joined me there. Now this is where the controversy begins. I believe he left Central State to follow me to University of Akron, but he insisted he transferred to my school because it was closer to home. To this day, he cannot admit he just wanted to be with me. I moved into the dorms, and he had an apartment off campus.

Our relationship was funny because we never officially got back together, but because we spent so much time together, no one knew the difference. We talked about getting married. I remember being at the school library one evening, and we decided that we would get engaged at Christmas. Which is exactly what happened. We finished that year and got married the following September. We have been inseparable ever since. Now about that proposal—although I knew the proposal was coming, I did not expect it to be as impromptu as it was. On Christmas Day, as usual, we spent time with both our parents. We were leaving his to go to mine. He was driving his parents in an Aerostar minivan. He reached over to hand me a ring box with bows on it. He did not stop driving. He did not look at me. He just mumbled out a proposal. It was not romantic in the least. But I knew how much he loved me, so I gladly accepted.

*****

Keith had a very close relationship with his mother. No, he is not a "momma's boy" in the traditional sense. However, they did make a point to talk or see each other every day. We would have awesome Sunday dinners at her home. We would talk, laugh, and generally have a great time with family. We would alternate between spending time with his family and mine. The best part of our marriage is that my family loves my husband. He is a son and brother to them, not an in-law. I am thankful to say, his family loves me. No "in-law drama" at all.

Imagine my surprise when my husband said to me one evening in 2003, "God said we are to relocate to Phoenix." My first thought was there is no way my husband will ever leave his mom (yes, they were that close).

I thought to myself, *Just give it time, this notion will pass.* However, I was wrong. In fact, it only got stronger.

He would look at me and say. "I'm serious, God said we are moving." He even began to make arrangements to leave his job. My husband had been a corrections officer for ten years at the time. I had been working at a local bank for about ten years as well. He was so convincing in his statement that I became concerned.

I was called into ministry in 1997. My husband also had a call of God on his life; however, at this time, he had not yet fully accepted it. I remember sitting in a minister's meeting at church and asking them to pray over the situation. Still in my mind, I thought I was not going anywhere unless God spoke to me directly. I truly believe no one took this proposed move seriously. They were all convinced that there was no way my husband would move so far away from his mom. My mother-in-law had been having some health issues. She needed to have a kidney transplant, and my husband had agreed to be the donor. All the required tests were done, and he was a match. They just needed to wait until she was medically cleared to proceed with the surgery. We had no idea how long it would take for her to be cleared. He would need to be available once she was strong enough for the procedure. However, Keith surprised us all. He stated, "I will just fly back when the time comes."

One day, my husband came home from work and informed me that he was scheduled to leave his job at the end of July 2003. I want to say I was blindsided by this news, but technically I was not. I just never believed it would happen. At this point, I really began to seek God. I remember going on a consecration seeking God's face over the situation. I was still fully determined not to go anywhere unless God revealed himself to me. I remember I was in my bedroom. I had the television on in the background, watching a *Bountiful Blessings* telecast with Bishop G. E. Patterson. And I was praying, and I heard God audibly saying, "You are moving." From that moment on, I was fully persuaded. It is amazing how God can just speak one or two words into you heart that will change your whole life. This is what happened to me. After that, I began to make preparations to pack up our home and move cross-country.

I remember my mother being so concerned and trying to talk me out of our move. If you have ever had God speak to you in such a dramatic way, there is really nothing anyone can say that will talk you out of doing just what he said. This was my case. I finally understood how my husband could move away from all that we have ever known for the unknown. And believe me, it was truly the unknown. All I had was a word from God. But that was all I needed. When God speaks, it is like fire shut up in my bones (Jeremiah 20:9). You cannot deny the call or pull of God. You will do what he said. I asked my husband why we were moving; he did not know. Simply said, God will reveal himself once we are there. For me, God did not tell me why, only that we are going. That was enough.

It has to be said, not everyone who is supposed to have your best interests at heart will understand the call on your life. You must have enough courage and trust in God to live. To live the life that God has planned, even if that means your life is thousands of miles away for all you know. I think of Abraham, how he had to leave to find what God had promised. Many times, it is necessary to move away from what is familiar to find your own voice and to stand on your own two feet. It is a way to mature and grow up. It is a way to step away from your comfort zone and trust God—for everything. You are in a place where no one can easily come to your rescue if you mess up.

Leaving my church was difficult. As I stated, we met and got married at the same church in which we grew up. We were choir members, and I served on the ministerial staff. A lot of memories, great church services, and wonderful friends were all tied to this church. Ultimately, the journey to leaving was heartbreaking. We had a goodbye party in which my pastor was not able to attend. She later stated she forgot about the party. The final Sunday before we left, I wanted to say my final goodbye to my pastor, and she had the nerve to ask me where I was going. Yes, that was heartbreaking. However, the choir gave us a loving tribute as a going-away that included a lovely plaque for our years of dedication. I remembered the word of the Lord, and I left with a smile on my face and love in my heart for the place where I grew up and learned how to minister to God's people. No, everyone does not understand God's plan for your life. We must lean into what God said and forget about the rest.

*****

In addition to my husband and I, we were blessed with two handsome sons, Kyle Jr. and D'Andre. We bought our home in 1998. We lived in a three-bedroom house in Lorain, Ohio. I remember cleaning my living room one Saturday morning, and the Lord saying to my heart, "This is not your home." I was so upset at the time that I went into denial and began rebuking the devil for the thought. I loved our home and took pride in it. I was not yet ready to embrace anything that would take it away. Now, looking back at that incident, I can testify that what he said was the truth; I just refused to receive it then. Looking back, I realize it was not the time. But God is faithful that he gives us plenty of warnings in advance. It also shows how God does have a plan for our lives. Most of the time, we do not fully understand the depth of what that plan is. We think that what we want our lives to be is the plan, and to some extent, it may be. However, the journey to get there is another matter. Unbeknownst to us, our journey was just beginning.

At the time of our move, our children were twelve and eight years old. I was able to go online and find a two-bedroom, two-bathroom apartment in Phoenix. Thank God for technology! I was able to view the apartment online, so I knew what it looked like. I was even able to research crime and schools in the area, so I was reasonably comfortable with our new home. We decided it would be better to sell or give away all that we had, with the exception of our computer and clothes. We would have to buy everything else once we arrived in Phoenix. We did not want to drive our car and a moving truck cross-country.

It is not easy giving up all the comforts of our old life. All of the stuff accumulated over years of marriage is a lot. We had to pick through our life memories and decide what we kept, what we gave away to family, and what we sold. It was tough on everyone. There were tons of stuff my boys wanted to keep, family photos and keepsakes, and stuff we used every day. But ultimately, we were able to whittle everything down to what would fit in the trunk of our Ford Taurus and part of the back seat, and we set out on our journey. It was a thirty-three-hour drive, but we planned to complete it in two to three days.

CHAPTER 2

Finding Solid Ground

Three days! A very long three-day road trip from Ohio to Phoenix in a packed Ford Taurus. After 2,007 miles, a hotel in Missouri, and another in Texas, we finally arrived in the city that would be home for the next twelve years. Fortunately, I was able to go online and locate an apartment in a decent area before we left Ohio. We just needed to sign the lease and pay the deposit and move in.

At the time of our move, our children were very young and away from all that was familiar. I was determined to make the transition as smooth as possible for them. I wanted to make breakfast and see my children on the school bus and be there for them when they got home. I was never a stay-at-home mom; this was a new experience for me. But this was more important than anything else for them, and I needed to do it right. We needed to find a new sense of normal, where they felt safe and supported.

This decision was proven to be the right one almost immediately; I remember getting a call from the school asking for a meeting with me to discuss my youngest son. My husband and I arrived not knowing what to expect. There were never any behavior issues with him at his previous school.

We arrived at his school, and I immediately understood the issue. There was hardly anyone in attendance at the school—children or teachers—that looked like my son. He is tall for his age and African American. The teacher was upset because she felt my son was clinging to her rather than making friends with the other Latin American and Caucasian children. In this previous experience, the student body was a fair mix of all three (and more). Being the only black child in his school was a culture shock for him.

In the meeting, the teacher went on to describe how abnormal my child was and stated she wanted to have my son tested for a learning disability. After being told by the principal that this teacher was one of his very best, I looked him in the eye and told him if she was his best, then the school sucked. After the shocked intake of breath, I explained that if a teacher could not understand how traumatic it is for a child to be thrown into a new school that was vastly different from what he had previously known, then she needed to go back to school. I then turned to the teacher and told her no, we will not allow them to label my son with a learning disability simply because she was not prepared to do her job effectively. I looked back at the principal and told him my son has an excellent support system at home, and we would aggressively advocate for him. I then politely asked to have my son moved to another class immediately.

After this meeting, I did more research and had my son enrolled in another school, where the student body was more diversified. I learned that day the importance of diversity. Everyone deserves to be represented and to feel welcomed and accepted. If we can teach our children this lesson when they are young, it will better prepare them for their adult life.

I would like to say that my son went on to be very involved with the student government in junior high and high school. He was even the president of the student body during his senior year. It is very important for a child to find something that peaks their interest and just get involved. He may have been thrown by culture shock initially, but he eventually found a way to thrive in the new environment. After the move to a new school, both of my boys were more settled, and I felt it safe to return to work. I was extremely fortunate that I worked for a national bank at the time. As part of my preparation to move, I search for a job within my company that would allow me to simply transfer. After a telephone interview with the branch manager, I was told to give him a call when I got to town. I was allowed extra time to get my family settled, then I was able to resume working. I did take a couple of months to make the call because we needed time to find solid ground.

My husband was able to find work almost immediately, but nothing like he had previously. He signed up with a security outfit and patrolled local businesses. Did I mention he worked the night shift? That is how I realized that I hate to sleep alone. Add to that being in a new city and a new apartment—I heard every sound there was to hear during the long nights. Needless to say, Phoenix, Arizona, was a culture shock for us all. We had to learn to quickly adapt to not only the weather but to the Phoenix way of life.

*****

It is amazing how God brings people into our lives to teach us or show us something that we desperately need at that time. This was the case for us, several times in fact. The first time was getting to know our upstairs neighbors, Nonna and her two beautiful daughters. The girls were a lot younger than our boys, but they quickly developed a bond. My sons were sort of their protectors from the other kids. Nonna was a nice but streetwise young mother, who did not mind doing what needed to be done to take care of her girls. She did have a boyfriend (the girl's dad), who was around, but I honestly cannot remember a whole lot about him.

As I said, we sold everything to make this move. So needless to say, we had no furniture to speak of. We had my computer, one DVD—*Bringing Down the House* with Steve Martin and Queen Latifa. We had a nice two-bedroom, two-bathroom apartment that was otherwise empty. But at this time, we only had the computer. Because my computer also had a CD/DVD player, we were able to watch that movie over and over again. I believe we must have watched that movie at least fifty times. Fortunately for us, we loved the movie. A friend of ours, who had made the same move years earlier, had eventually offered us the use of his daughter's bedroom television.

After Nonna found out about the DVD, she told us we could get a public library card and rent DVDs there for free. The best part, the library was right down the street, and we never noticed it. We were so excited to add variety to our DVD options, but mostly we were just glad that we did not have to watch that movie again. To this day, whenever I see that movie playing on television, I am taken right back to our time in Phoenix. Yes, it is a fond memory. She also told us about a program that the local Catholic charities had that would give us vouchers to get furniture for our apartment. She walked us through the application process and helped us rent a truck to collect the furniture too. I know this seems simple or common knowledge. But as I said before, my husband and I come from large families. We were the youngest, so we did not have to concern ourselves with these types of things. Our older siblings would take care of it. This is one of the benefits of a large family.

We were able to furnish our apartment with everything we needed. Shortly after this happened, Nonna moved, and we never heard from them again. Some people mourn when people leave our lives for whatever reason. We cannot afford to get caught up in who has gone away. We must learn to embrace the experiences, the lessons we learned, and the added value they brought to us or just appreciate the blessings we received while they were there. God has a way of sending what we need through unexpected channels. We need to learn to recognize what God has done, be thankful, and keep it moving.

My husband got our boys involved with the local Boys & Girls Club of America. This turned out to be a brilliant move. My boys were able to meet a lot of kids their own age and engage in sports and other fun activities. They were able to make, what would turn out to be, lifelong friends. Bonus, a lot of the kids attended the same schools, so they did not have to feel they were at the school alone anymore. It was very different from life in Ohio, but we were finding solid ground.

God showed himself to be faithful in orchestrating ordinary things to bring us to solid ground. Normal life was taking shape for our family. I was able to phase seamlessly back into my career. My husband hated the security job and was able to eventually fall into a totally different line of work. He realized he was very good at sales then eventually became an enrollment advisor at a local college. Our life in Phoenix was beginning to take shape.

CHAPTER 3

Walking Headfirst into Purpose

Whoever said finding your purpose would lead to happiness and personal fulfillment is nuts! Well, I guess it would depend on the context of the discovery. In our case, purpose would unravel or reveal itself in a frightening way.

For us, it began late one evening in our bedroom in 2008.

My husband told me he was not feeling well and asked me what heartburn felt like. I used to have bad bouts of heartburn frequently and must have complained about it often. I explained that I usually have an uncomfortable burning sensation in my chest area and sometimes a little nausea. He told me to go back to sleep, and he went into the bathroom. He came out shortly and stated he was going to go to the emergency room, and no, he did not want me to drive him. He would call me if it was something serious.

Let me just interject here: Keith had a bad habit of treating the emergency room as his primary doctor. Instead of making an appointment, he would run to the local emergency room for treatment. This was before there was an urgent care center on every corner. So when he said he was heading to the hospital, I didn't think anything of it.

Unknown to us both, this was the beginning of finding out why God sent us to Phoenix.

The news from the emergency room was devastating. Keith was admitted into the hospital because they were concerned about his heart. A day later, he had to have an exploratory surgery, a heart catheterization. This is a procedure where they take a look at the heart to check all the major arteries for blockage and the overall health of the heart. Before he went in to have the procedure, we prayed and agreed that we were going to stand on faith for his healing and trust God.

My children were both at school, and I was in the waiting room alone, waiting patiently for the surgeon to come out and give me an update. In my mind, I was preparing myself for the news that Keith had some minor blockage that could be corrected surgically and maintained with a proper diet. However, I was not prepared for the news that I received.

The doctor did indeed come out to speak with me. But he was terrible at delivering news. I felt like I was one in a long line that needed to be given an update so he could move on to the next patient. Initially, there was very little compassion in his delivery. He called for the family, and when I raised my hand, he came over. His head was down looking at paperwork, and he delivered news that shook my world. He told me my husband had a lot of fluid buildup around his heart, and there was a 65 percent chance that he would not survive. Then it looked as if he was going to walk away. I gasped out loud and asked him to slowly repeat what he just said. It was at that point that he actually looked at me. He then noticed the effect his words had on me and finally expressed compassion and empathy. I like to tell myself that he was busy and was just trying to get on with a busy day.

But at some point, medical professionals need to realize what they deal with on a daily basis is earth-shattering to the people who are intimately involved. We are not used to this and need time to wrap our minds around the news they have to give. The doctor rebounded well and gave me the time I needed to understand what he was saying.

Keith had to have a second surgery a few days later. They placed a defibrillator on his heart to shock it if it ever got out of rhythm. Needless to say, getting through airport security was never the same again.

This surgery took place in 2008 but was the first of many more to come.

It was sometime later that my husband shared with me his bathroom experience on the night he first went to the emergency room. He told me God told him there was a problem with his heart and to get up and go to the emergency room. Then he told me something that I have held onto ever since. Keith said, "God told me not to worry because I would never die from heart issues, but to get up and go to the emergency room." Hearing this promise of God gave me peace. I embraced this word just as God spoke it directly to my own heart. I stand on it even now, years later.

One thing I found to be true in my walk with God is never let go of the things he speaks directly to my heart. No matter what happens in my life, I trust the words that he took the time to speak to me. It is like being given the answers to the test or given the key to the lock at the beginning of trouble. I know that no matter what, this trouble is not the end of me. I will survive and thrive. This does not mean the journey is easy. However, there is a sense of well-being in the midst of trouble. An attitude that says, yes, I am going through, but it will be alright. That was my attitude as Keith and I walked through this journey together. Yes, it was frightening at times. Many days I felt a numbness in my emotions. But God delivered me every time. I could not afford to fall apart. I had a family who needed me to stand.

We soon realized why we needed to be away from home. It would have been impossible to deal with this situation with both of our families intimately involved in every decision we would need to face. My husband's siblings are very dramatic, but they love their brother dearly. His mother would have not been able to see her son in such a vulnerable state. But God, in his infinite wisdom, did what needed to be done. He moved us across the country.

After the surgery, God really began to deal with Keith about the call that he placed on his life. My husband is an anointed preacher and a pastor. He ran from this pull on his life for many years. However, God had to get him to a place where he could no longer run. God put him into a situation where he needed to sit still, hear from him, and trust him. God began to give Keith visions of his ministry and gave him a peek at the road map of our life. This is why I appreciate God the most. God told my husband that once this was all over, we would then need to go to North Carolina to begin our ministry. But unlike the first time, God shared this news with me as well.

God is amazing. He allows us to experience some peace or relief before he hits us with more trouble. Such was the case with our journey. Because of Keith's illness, he was not always able to work. This caused a financial burden on our family. While he was dealing with his recovery, I had to make some tough decisions. We had to downsize from two vehicles to one, and we had to move into an apartment that I could afford on my own salary if need be. Fortunately, I was able to find a place that was right across the street from my son's elementary school and down the street the high school our oldest attended.

Keith was never forthcoming with me regarding the pain he was in on a daily basis. When he was able to go back to work, he found a new job where he could take the city bus. There was no way he would allow me to take the bus. He insisted that I drive the car, and he would deal with the city bus. I will never fully understand what a challenge this was for him. It would be several years later when he confessed that there were days when he did not know if he would survive the grueling chore of running to catch a bus, then not finding a seat, and standing for the ride that involved several transfers just to make it to North Phoenix—we lived in Central Phoenix at the time. Then walk from the bus stop to his office. Repeating the same journey in the opposite direction at the end of the day. This took a toll on him.

When he did finally tell me, it made me love him even more. He was trying to look out for me even when he was very sick. God truly blessed me with a great husband, and I do know what a blessed woman I am. It is funny, I remember telling a good friend of mine how much I appreciated the anointing that was on her life, but I never wanted to go through the things she did to walk in it. The words she said to me have never left me. She said, "If you don't want to go through the fire, you will never get to what God has for you." I sat there thinking about that for a long time. God quietly ushered us into this journey, literally taking us to the desert of Phoenix so we could go through the fire he had ordered just for us. We were walking headfirst into our purpose, and we did not even fully know it.

CHAPTER 4

They Say Ignorance Is Bliss

You never know how strong you are until you face a situation in which you are not allowed to fall apart. You literally have so many people who need you, who requires you to push aside your own feelings of despair so you can be someone else's rock.

I witnessed my husband be the rock that his siblings needed while dealing with the illness and subsequent passing of my father-in-law. A great man whom we lovingly called Pops.

Keith had the defibrillator in place when we found out that my father-in-law was in hospice care. Let me just say, God truly takes care of his children, even in sickness. Our family called us home, to see him before he passed away. We flew back home to Ohio. As we made our way to the hospice facility, we were preparing ourselves for the worse. But as we entered his room, it was to find Pops sitting up in bed, clothed in his cotton pajamas with a remote control in his hand, watching television. He did not look sick at all. He looked just as he had when we would visit him at his home.

As we were talking, he told us how wonderful people had been to him. How they would visit and sing his favorite gospel songs and pray with him. He did not have one complaint or one bad word about his situation or how he was feeling. I truly admired this great man.

The family did not know that Pops had been sick for a long time. He never told anyone what he was going through. We were all ignorant to his silent pain. The family interacted with Pops on a daily basis, yet no one knew he had colon cancer. My mother-in-law had a long illness that Pops did his best to see her through. He was a rock for her to the point where he was not concerned with his own health.

We visited with him a few times before we headed back to Phoenix. Pops passed away a few weeks later. We again headed back to Ohio to assist in preparation for his funeral.

*****

My mother-in-law was sick at the same time as Pops. I believe the reason why we were ignorant of Pops's illness is because we were all so engrossed with getting Mother J back on her feet. Mom was dealing with many health issues, mainly kidney failure and heart issues. Before we moved away, Keith and Pops would take Mother J to her appointments at the Cleveland Clinic together. For some reason, Pops loved to have Keith drive them, and his favorite thing was to enjoy a meal at the hospital cafeteria on these trips.

Prior to his illness, Keith had planned to donate a kidney to Mother J. At one point, he even flew back to Ohio to have the surgery. Unfortunately, it was during the testing for the procedure when Mother J was diagnosed with cancer that would prevent the surgery from taking place. It is ironic how we make plans to do things, but God had other ideas.

A few years later, Mother J had a stroke and was placed on life support. After a time, the doctors advised us to disconnect life support. They stated it was only the system that was keeping Mom alive. But Mother J surprised everyone and continued to breathe on her own, even after everything was disconnected. It was during this time that Pops passed away.

*****

We flew back to Ohio.

My loving in-laws are a dramatic and emotional bunch. For some reason, they all looked to my husband for balance. He was the voice of reason. A calming presence in a chaotic time. He became the rock they needed to navigate these difficult days. It was at this time that I realized how we were able to miss Pop's illness. My husband was very sick, but he would only allow me to see just how physically weak he really was. He showed strength to everyone else.

We stayed with my parents while we were in town. During the day, we would travel to the funeral home to help plan the services. But when we got back home, the cracks would show. He would be the voice of reason when everyone was arguing during the planning. At night, I would hold him as he dealt with the stress and pain.

On the day of the funeral, we all banded together, celebrating this great man, husband, and father who was Pops. We buried him in a mixture of sorrow and joy. We would miss his presence in our lives. But he was now in Abraham's bosom and free from pain. We spent time with our extended family and friends at the repass, where we got to share fond memories with Pops. The sad part was Mother J was not there. She was unaware of what was going on with her beloved Curly (that is what she called him). Her absence was felt by us all.

When we got back to my parents' house, we were preparing for our return trip home to Phoenix. My husband began to take a turn for the worse. I had to cajole him into taking a visit to see his mom. He told me he was too sick to do it. But I knew, if something were to happen to her and he missed this opportunity to see her again, he would never forgive himself. I told him this as well. It was enough to get him up and moving. We were able to visit Mother J one last time before heading home. Keith was able to kiss her face and tell her how much she was loved.

Unfortunately, Keith became really sick, and we had to make a trip to the emergency room.

It's funny how it is the people you least expect are the ones to come through when you are in need. While Keith and I were sitting in his hospital room in Ohio, trying to figure out our next move, we had an unexpected visit. This beautiful sister and her two friends heard we were in the hospital; they came up to encourage and pray with us. Now mind you, everyone knew we were in the hospital, but none of them came to check on us. Not my family nor his. But this sister did. We grew up together. She was the little sister of one of our good friends. She came with her anointed oil and prayed. We all talked for a while, and they prayed for our safe journey home. Keith and I decided, no matter what, we needed to get home. And home was now in Phoenix. We discharged him against medical advice to catch our flight.

This was the best decision we could have made. God sent us to Phoenix. We may not have understood why we were there at the time, but we were determined to follow God. To walk in obedience.

One thing I have learned, it is better to be in the will of God than not. The Bible we know in part. The one part we did understand is that our blessing was in Phoenix. Our provision was there. We needed to be there to fulfill the will of God for our lives.

Some of our family and friends were upset that we got on the plane back to Phoenix. They felt we should have just stayed there in the hospital. I believe they were thinking about what was convenient for them or what was better for them. We had to think about what God said to us. We had to choose to walk in that and forget about the rest.

I do not regret that decision, not even a little.

CHAPTER 5

Holding on to God's Promise
(When They Give Up, You Don't)

They say there is no place like home! And I believe this is true, but sometimes going home leads you straight into the fire. This was our experience coming back home to Phoenix. It was great to be home because we were able to see our boys (they did not travel with us to Ohio). It was a fire because Keith was still very sick.

After a day or so, we found ourselves back in the hospital. Keith had gotten sick during the night, so we took an all-too-familiar journey to the emergency room.

It is confession time. I must admit to giving in to my feelings of frustration and venting to my husband. It was late at night midweek, and I had to get up for work early. At this point, my husband was not able to work because he was so very weak, and his bad days (health-wise) were far outweighing the good ones. Technically he was employed but had to miss a lot of days. The financial responsibility for our family staying afloat was on my shoulders, so to miss work was not an option for me. My husband had a habit of refusing to go to the hospital on the weekends because he wanted to enjoy that time with his family. He would wait until the weekdays to go to the emergency room. I do understand his thought process, but I felt that he never saw it from my point of view.

Anyhow, this frustration of mine built up to the level that I had to verbally express myself. I was driving to the emergency room about 12:30 a.m., and I was stopped at a traffic light. I turned to Keith and said, "At some point, you are going to have to walk by faith and trust God for your healing." It was the look on his face, when he turned to me, that had me realize how foolish I sounded. It was not as if he wasn't walking by faith, but his symptoms were so severe that lying down in bed made them worse. To him, this was the worst part of the day, mixed with weakness and fatigue, which at times took its toll. He was diagnosed with congestive heart failure at this point. It was more comfortable to sit up rather than to lie down.

This particular trip to the emergency room was the beginning of the end. Although we did not know it at the time.

I must reiterate, at no time did I believe that Keith would die. I believed the promise God gave to Keith when we started this journey; He promised he would not die from a heart issue. And we were definitely dealing with heart issues!

Keith was admitted to the hospital and was on the cardiac floor. As usual, they did a gauntlet of tests, checking everything they could, but the results were all the same. I remember sitting in his room one evening and looking at the faces of the staff as they would come in and out of the room. No one would give me a clear understanding of what was going on. I remember one nurse in particular who would just speak soothingly to us both, and I could see the pity in his eyes.

The doctors would speak with my husband during the day while I was at work. When I would come in the evenings, he was so out of it from the pain medication that he could not remember everything they would tell him. With the exception of one thing, there was one doctor who knew a cardiologist at the Mayo Clinic in Phoenix. He was going to ask to have that doctor review Keith's case. I heard nothing else about that.

Finally, I was walking past the nursing station on my way back from the bathroom. I heard them remarking they were keeping him comfortable until he passed away because there was nothing else that could be done. I was not sure if they were talking about my husband or not. When the nurse came into the room again, I asked him point blank; he confirmed that was accurate.

Now I must stop here and say when everyone else gives up, don't you! Keep holding onto what God said over everyone else, no matter what everyone else is saying. Whether it is mom, dad, brother, sister, cousin, or friend. If it be teacher, boss, lawyer, or judge—no matter what they say, believe what God says over them! God will never fail you or let you down. My husband was in this hospital for close to a month, and all they were doing was making him comfortable until he died. But I was praying, and I had a list of prayer warriors praying with me back in Ohio.

It is funny, when God is working, the enemy is attacking on every hand. I came into my husband's room to find him very upset. I mentioned earlier that my in-laws are very dramatic. I found out that they kept calling my husband's room and upsetting him. They would be on the phone crying and carrying on to the point where the staff pulled me aside to tell me they could not have them upsetting him. I had to instruct them not to let him speak to any of them. He did not need to deal with how they felt over his sickness. For some reason, the family did not call me or my sons at home. They would only call Keith at the hospital. This helped me understand that our journey had to take us away from Ohio. It would have been too difficult to control the situation if we were still there; God knew exactly what we needed to survive this journey.

I learned another lesson as well: I understood why God would often call his people away from what is familiar toward the unknown. To truly grow, we must face our own personal desert places, where all we have is God to lean on. This causes us to trust him on a level we never have previously.

A few days later, I was told by one of the doctors that my husband's case was being reviewed by Mayo Clinic. If he was found to be a candidate for a heart transplant, they would transfer him to Mayo Clinic for ongoing care. I remember initially meeting Dr. Steidley, and he told me they would take the case because he was confident they could help him. I was excited that my husband would now get some help instead of just being drugged. I agreed to the transfer. All I asked was that they not transfer him without letting me know, and Dr. Steidley agreed. However, even in this, there was drama. I went to the hospital to visit my husband only to find he was not there. Yes, I freaked out a little. They had moved my husband without letting me know. With tearful anxiety, I had to pursue after him. This was my first introduction to the Mayo Clinic in Phoenix, Arizona.

It is amazing what we must go through to get where God needs us to be. All it takes is someone with vision. Vision to see past who or what you are now to what you can be. God knew what he was doing. With this whole team of doctors providing care, and the many nurses and technicians carrying out the orders and treatment, there was only one doctor who had enough foresight to contact a specialist at another hospital. This is no criticism of the hospital staff. They did their jobs well and provided great care for my husband. The problem was that they could not do more. If it had not been for that one doctor with vision, the end could be disastrous. But God orders our steps. He strategically places and positions us to receive.

Hindsight is a wonderful thing. Now I can look back and see all the areas of our life where God was moving on our behalf. Back then, all I could do was hold on to the promise of God. I trusted he would complete the work he started. That he would not put more on me (us) than we could bear. That he would never leave nor forsake us.

Most times while we are in the center of our desert place, it is almost impossible to have vision beyond what we are going through at this moment. The best we can do is view the steps that are right in front of us and make prayerful decisions. Trusting the God that is ordering our steps.

CHAPTER 6

Hospital Life

Inhale, exhale. Again, inhale, exhale. Hospital life allowed me to breathe. It was a relief to have Keith in a hospital whose goal was to fix him and get him well. Instead of being in a place where their goal was to make him comfortable until he died. We were a team, and life at Mayo Clinic allowed me to breathe.

However, hospital life was not without its challenges. Keith was in a private room, where we could bring pictures from home and a CD player to play music that would uplift him during those lonely times. Unfortunately, no matter how comfortable the surroundings, his physical situation remained the same. At this point, his situation was beginning to take its toll on his ability to eat food as well as his mental health. He had already been in the first hospital for a month—away from our sons, his friends, and the social interactions he was used to.

About the second week of residence at Mayo Clinic in Phoenix, Arizona, one of the doctors pulled me aside. He explained that my husband was not eating. If he continued not to eat, they would need to put in a feeding tube. If this was done, then he would no longer be eligible for a transplant. At this point, he was not yet officially listed on the transplant registry. They were still testing and evaluating him to make this determination. As I entered his room, I sat down and explained the situation. I picked up the spoon and began to feed him. He looked me in the eye and opened his mouth. We agreed that together, we are going to do whatever we need to get him back home to our children and regular life. He did not eat a great deal that day, but he did make a conscious effort to eat more at each meal.

This taught me a lesson. There are times when we may not feel like doing what is necessary. Or that we may not have the time to do what is necessary. But if we don't make the effort or take the time, we will lose the most important things in our lives and wonder how it happened. Keith's sickness was robbing him of his appetite. Because his health was in such a poor state, he could not afford not to eat. Proper food and nutrition is a key factor in any recovery. We prayed and he ate. He worked at eating every day. Soon enough, the talk of a feeding tube was no more.

Just when I thought we were coasting along, here comes another mini-crisis.

At this point, Keith had been evaluated, and he qualified to be placed on the transplant list. He was not at the top of the list, but he was on it. A few weeks later, I was again on my way to see my husband; I was pulled aside again. This time, they were wondering if Keith was mentally stable to be on the transplant list. They were worried because he always seemed confused when they would come into his room.

Let me stop here to mention that a person's mental health can be severely impacted by a prolonged illness. Stress, anxiety, and depression are common. However, depending on the medical history, post-traumatic stress disorder, or PTSD, may be common as well. If you find yourself dealing with any mental health issues, please self-care and find appropriate treatment. Understand that no one is going to care for your well-being as much as you do. Be proactive and find help. There is no embarrassment in taking steps to ensure you are healthy, both mentally and physically.

In my husband's case, he gets nervous when there are a lot of people in a room and asks him question after question. Mayo Clinic is a teaching hospital (I believe). So when the team of doctors would come to see him, there would be a representative from each medical specialty involved in the transplant team. Each asking him questions that would help them with their part of the transplant process. Unfortunately, my husband would be in this alone because I had to work to financially care for our family. I was not able to come to him until after work.

We had to explain how these question-and-answer sessions made him a little anxious. I asked that they wait until I was able to be present, or if they could just ask me instead of my husband. Once we were able to get this pattern down, the question of his mental stability ceased. For some reason, professionals have a hard time understanding or seeing things from the eyes of the people they serve. Things that seem reasonable or simple to us sometimes go over their heads. Fortunately, we were able to overcome this crisis too.

*****

Sickness has a way of revealing how people really feel about you.

Hospital life was challenging, but God always placed great people in our life. As I may have mentioned, God relocated our family from Ohio to Arizona. We had only one close friend in the area. Shawn had also moved from Ohio a few years before we did. He and his family. My husband was in need of a barber but was very particular about whom he allowed to cut and shave him. Shawn and my husband went to the same barber shop. When the barber learned that Keith wanted a shave and a cut, he and Shawn made a visit to my husband. This simple act made Keith's day. I remember Keith telling me how the barber gave him the best service even with tears in his eyes. Shawn and my husband both tried to pay for the barber's time. But he refused. He just wanted to be of service. I thank God for that. It may seem weird, but it was a blessing to Keith, to Shawn, and to the barber. As the Bible says, it truly is better to give than receive. This experience—even many years later—still stands out to them all as they still speak of it in the face of the miracle God worked through the transplant.

Hospital life was completely different from being at home, but it still allowed us to have a new sense of normal. The days passed as we waited for a matching heart to become available.

I would just like to take a moment to thank everyone who decides to become an organ donor. It is amazing how many people are in need. It takes an awesome, selfless person to decide that when I am no longer using my organs, please give them to someone in need. To me, this is amazing! When you consider receiving a heart, it means someone else had to die to make it possible. I must confess prior to my husband's health crisis, I never really considered organ donation. However, after it happened, I immediately updated my donation status on my driver's license when it was time to renew. I wanted to be a blessing to someone and their family, just as my family was blessed.

My boys looked forward to seeing their dad. They were able to share the day's happenings with him, and Keith was able to feel a part of their lives again. They were not able to see Keith every day. But I made sure to bring them to the hospital two to three times each week. I wanted my boys to do as much of their normal daily activities as possible and still see their dad frequently. They were able to speak to him on the phone daily. This helped us all acclimate to hospital life.

CHAPTER 7

It's Okay to Ask for Help

Help comes in many forms. It does not always come in the shape or package that we imagined, but it always speaks to our situation. So it is important to recognize help when it comes.

I remember getting a call late at night from the hospital. It was a school night, so me and my sons were getting ready for bed. It was about 10:30 p.m. The caller was explaining to me that my husband's condition had taken a turn for the worse, and it was necessary to remove his heart and replace it with an artificial one. They told me to get there as soon as possible. I told them I was on my way and bringing my sons with me.

I did not know why, but I wanted my sons to see their father before the surgery.

I remember getting to the hospital; my husband was unconscious, lying in the bed. He was naked except for a white cloth covering him from beneath his chin down the center of his body. His arms and legs were uncovered. He was so small.

As long as I live, I will never forget seeing him that way. Now I think back and remember the goodness of God. To see how far God has brought him.

I walked into the room with my sons; Kyle Jr. was about seventeen, and D'Andre was about thirteen. The hospital staff was quiet, and so were we. I was just trying to take everything in. I looked over at my boys, to make sure they were okay. Kyle looked at me and said, "Mom, I can't take this. I'm going to step out." D'Andre was just quietly looking around. As Kyle left the room, he took D'Andre with him. Through this whole process, Kyle took charge of D'Andre to allow me to focus on their dad. I was so proud of him; he truly was becoming the man his dad raised him to be. D'Andre listened to him without complaint.

Although I was apprehensive, I reached down to take Keith's hand, and I prayed. This was hard for me. Not to pray—for I have always trusted God throughout this process. If we are honest with ourselves, it is the fear of the unknown that sometimes gets the better of us. But the hard part was seeing beyond this moment. God, what is the next step? In my case, I saw my husband, and I knew the major surgery he was about to have. Everything sort of hit me at once. I needed help! My boys needed me to stay strong. They needed me to be their rock or anchor that would keep us from floating away, and I needed help.

I remember sitting in the family waiting room in a recliner. I took out my phone and called home to Ohio. I had to call his family and mine, to let them know what was going on. I needed to speak with someone who knew how to pray. Because me and my family needed help. I remember speaking with our cousin Sian. She is a praying woman and an anointed Evangelist. I asked her to fly out to Phoenix to be with us. She agreed and was making plans. Then she said to me, "Just call your mom. Have her come and stay with you for a little while. Talk to her and call me back. I will make the flight arrangements for her."

At that moment, I realized I equated asking my mother to come was the same as asking for help. For whatever reason, I did not want to ask for help. This was foolish thinking. At some point, everyone needs help. Refusing to ask for help does not show strength. It does the opposite; it keeps you weak.

I picked up the phone and called my mother. I remember asking her to come and started crying. She said, "Yes, of course." The tears were of relief because I knew that there would be someone there with me to help bear this burden. I called my sister Mary. She told me she was glad Mom was coming out because she had already decided that she was coming so I would not be alone. This made me feel better. It is a blessing to know we do not have to go through trouble alone. All we have to do is ask for help. It is okay.

*****

The surgery was done in November 2009, and it took several long hours to complete.

As the transplant team explained to me, they would be taking out the majority of his natural heart. They would need to keep a portion of the top of his heart because they needed something to tether to the artificial heart. He was being placed on Big Blue, which would be attached to him with several thick tubes. Big Blue would function as his heart until a donor for a permanent heart could be found.

After the surgery was completed, I remember going into his room and hearing the machine beating like a heartbeat. It was indeed a big blue machine. It was about four feet tall and about four feet wide and was on wheels so he could be mobile. Eventually, Keith would be able to manuever around as the hospital staff pushed the machine to the restroom or different places in the hospital.

I remember when Keith became conscious, he looked at me and said, "That was the best sleep that I have had in a long time." He felt a lot better because his heart actually worked. It would take a lot of getting used to. I must admit, it was disconcerting to audibly hear his heartbeat continuously. Whenever I would hug him, I could feel the beats too. But I must say, the momentary discomfort was worth it to have my husband alive longer to wait for a permanent heart.

*****

My mother came to town. Mom is a retired nurse. She was a LPN for forty-one years in the same hospital back home.

She looked over everything to make sure they were in order. She asked intelligent questions regarding Keith's care and what we should expect. It was a great relief having her there. She saw to the boys because I still had to work to support us and pay for health insurance so my husband could have medical care. She also made my husband smile. He loved knowing that his family had help, if only for a little while. She cleaned our apartment and fixed meals and would go to the hospital with us. I was blessed with a truly great person for my mother. She made me glad that I did ask for help.

The hospital staff respected my mother too. When they knew we were on our way to visit, they would make sure everything was in its place. My mom wanted to make sure her son got the best care and was not afraid to point out anything she thought was amiss. Ultimately, she got to know the staff well. This helped us all feel comforted.

Shortly after my mother went back home, I received a call from my sister-in-law with very sad news. My mother-in-law had passed away. I was not sure how I could break the news to my husband. He was very close to his mom and had just gone through a major surgery. I decided to ask the social worker at the hospital for her advice on the best way to break the news to him. I honestly cannot remember what she advised because as I entered the room, Keith already knew what I needed to tell him. I did say the difficult words that needed to be said. His response to me was somehow he already knew. He believed God allowed her to stay with us until he successfully came through the surgery. Then she went on to be with the Lord.

Going through this journey has taught me that at some point in our lives, we all need help. The most healthy thing we can do is not be ashamed to ask for it and to be strong enough to accept it when it is offered. For me, getting helped saved my life.

CHAPTER 8

Sometimes a Distraction Is a Godsend

There is a saying "An idle mind is the devil's workshop." When my mind was not actively engaged, the reality of my situation would seep in. My mind would focus on the fact that my husband must live in the hospital to survive. My eyes would see the tubes coming from his chest and stomach going to Big Blue, his temporary heart. My ears would hear Big Blue pumping loudly as his heart. My hands would notice the difference in the feel of his skin as I touched him. My heart would leap to defend him and be prepared to fight every battle he needed fought. I lived a life of vigilance. This was an exhausting state to be in. Honestly, who could sustain it without becoming overwhelmed?

This state of play, if left unchecked, would cause even the strongest person to become mentally and physically weak. Weakness was something I could not afford. My husband needed me to step up and be strong for the family we created together. Let me just say, yes, traditional roles do dictate that in a relationship, the male is strong for the female and their children. He covers and provides for them, but it is important to remember, we are designed to work together. It was my turn to step in to cover and provide for our family. It was his time to lean on me. I was determined to be the strength he needed.

I was surprised at the reaction of people when they learned of my husband's illness. So many people were surprised that I would stay with Keith while he was going through this health crisis. Truthfully, I was surprised at how many people would leave their mate to deal with the situation alone. Our wedding vows said, "In sickness and in health, for richer or poorer, till death do us part." I (we) took our vows seriously. So yes, this was happening to us, not just to him. We are in this relationship together.

Distractions were a godsend. In my case, the distraction saved my life.

A perfect example of working together in a relationship, about six months before my husband got sick, he encouraged me to go back to school to finish my degree. Keith understood how important my education was to me, and he also understood I did not want to put a financial burden on our family. I did not want to take on extra debt. Keith convinced me to quit making excuses and just go back to school. Little did he know, this decision helped to save my sanity!

Because I had to work to support our family, my routine would be to work eight hours, head home to fix dinner for our sons, and then head over to Mayo Clinic. I would spend a few hours with Keith then head home to rest. Keith must have noticed how tired I was. He encouraged me to bring my laptop with me to the hospital. I would do homework while he watched television. Then we would have time to just talk. There was a freedom in losing myself in my studies. Schoolwork allowed my mind to have a break from my reality. It was an escape. I must admit, because my schedule took a toll on me, I was really tired at times. There were many days when I would sit at the hospital with my husband, laptop opened on my lap in the recliner, and I would just sleep. It was comforting to be there with him and rest. Yes, I would need to do work when I got home, but that was okay. Being with him gave me comfort and peace; I was able to rest.

However, when I was at home again, lying in my bed at night, missing my husband's presence, reality would come back with full force. This is when the tears would come and when frustrations materialized. I knew that I could not and would not make it through without God. But I must be honest, it was hard for me to pray. This is when I felt the prayers that people were praying on our behalf. The only thing I could do was lie there and rest my mind. I felt the prayers because I never missed work, and I never missed going to sit with Keith. I never missed an assignment; my children had home-cooked meals. Yes, the prayers of the people of God were keeping us afloat.

*****

My husband's mental status had greatly improved. They were allowing him to do more. Mayo Clinic had what they called cooking therapy. This gave Keith the opportunity to leave his room and go into the kitchen and cook meals for a few of the staff. This distraction helped him forget for a short time the seriousness of his condition and tediousness of his daily routine. This new therapy allowed him to mentally escape and find joy in something else. It opened up his social circle, and he was able to see different people. This new therapy gave him room to just breathe and relax.

I would bring the boys to see him a few times each week, and we would try to spend most weekends with him. He wanted to find a way to take care of us. It was hard for him to relinquish this responsibility that he took so seriously.

To me, He would find ways to feed us while we were there with him. Money was tight, and it was not always possible for us to buy hospital cafeteria food. He would talk with the social worker at the hospital, to get food vouchers for us. I told him this was not necessary; we could eat at home before we came. But he insisted. It became clear to me that this was something he needed to do. I realized I needed to let him do this so he can provide for us.

This is the importance of distracting your mind. A clear mind brought my husband back; a clear mind saved my sanity. It is impossible to be in an emotionally, physically, and financially charged situation without something to distract and occupy your mind. Embrace the distraction. It will allow you to continue to function at a high level in the midst of the stress you must face.

With a clear mind, I was able to pray for myself again. I still had a hard time sleeping without Keith beside me, but I was okay. I was able to just sit and enjoy spending time with my husband. We would just be together and enjoy it. We had the promise of God that he was going to complete the work of healing. Keith was going to get a heart. We were just waiting on the promise of God, and we were able to do it in the peace of God.

I'll say it again, the right kind of distractions can bring peace to a stressful situation. I still enjoy reading as a way to decompress. I recommend everyone find a hobby that helps them to relax and relieve stress. A hobby can help to improve mental health.

CHAPTER 9

The Sad/Happy News

Not all late-evening telephone calls are bad.

It is a common belief that when the phone rings late at night means something terrible has happened. Definitely something unexpected. Most of us dread those calls, as if good things only happen in daylight. However, in our case, this late telephone call was both happy and sad news.

I remember lying in my bed this particular night. The boys were both in their room asleep—they were to go to school the next morning. I was off work because Monday was a holiday—Martin Luther King Jr. Day. I was not yet asleep. I had the television on, not really paying attention to the show that was playing. So when the phone rang, I answered not knowing what to expect. I remember it was Dr. Steidley calling to tell me to get to the hospital as soon as possible. They found a heart that was a perfect match for Keith, and they were going to do the surgery. They wanted us to have a few minutes with Keith before they took him in to get his new heart.

Truthfully, I don't know how I felt. I was a little numb.

I remember when they had put my husband on Big Blue, they told us we would not have to wait long for a heart.

They explained that because we were approaching the holiday season (Thanksgiving, Christmas, and New Year's), there would be someone drinking and driving, and it was inevitable that something would be available. That is hard to hear, but unfortunately, it is also true.

We did not concentrate on that. Our focus was on dealing with our new reality that included Big Blue. So when Thanksgiving passed without news and Christmas came without any updates, we just sort of settled into life as we knew it, struggling at times to stay positive and to stand in faith. Learning to trust God no matter the circumstance takes time and practice. We had to consciously choose to lean on God and not be swayed by our circumstances. I may have said it before—hospital life was very, very challenging!

When my husband would get down, the great nursing staff would encourage him as best they could; they were always very positive. After the Christmas season was over, they told us our best chance would be New Year's. So when New Year's came and went, we were still there with Big Blue as our constant friend and reminder. It reminded us that God was not done with us. It reminded us that God was able to keep us and to sustain us. God did that beautifully. But it was still a hard situation. Yes, New Year's had passed, and we were approaching another holiday.

When I got this call, I woke up my children. They were strong young men now; Kyle was a senior in high school, and D'Andre was a freshman. We got dressed and made our way to the Mayo Clinic in Phoenix. In the car, they asked tons of questions, but mainly it was a quiet ride. We were all dealing with our feelings and emotions in our own way. It was a lot to wrap our minds around. We hoped and prayed for this day for so long. And now it was here.

We were happy because my husband was getting a heart. My children would once again have their dad back home very soon. I would have my lover and best friend back home. Our life would go on (all glory to God). Our family would be back together under the same roof. We would be able to say goodbye to hospital life forever. But that was only one side of the coin.

I was sad because I understood for him to get that heart, someone had to lose their life. My family could only be reunited in this way because someone else's family would be suffering a huge loss. They were selfless enough to decide to give his or her organs to others so they could live. I understood what an awesome gift this is.

We hear about transplants all the time—kidney, liver, eye, tissue, etc.—but we must never forget the caring people who decided to become donors. These truly are life-giving, life-prolonging gifts to people they may never meet. It takes a special type of individual to elect to become an organ donor. My family and I are forever grateful to Keith's heart donor and their family.

*****

When we got to the hospital, I remember walking into Keith's room. He was in a gown standing up next to Big Blue, and there was a male nurse standing with him. The nurse asked me if I was glad to be saying goodbye to old Blue. I smiled at my husband, and I said, "Yes, I am." I remember the look on Keith's face. We were both happy, excited, and apprehensive at the same time. We said a prayer asking God to be in the surgery and guide the hands of everyone involved. I left the room, and I and the boys went down to the surgical waiting area.

It was a very long surgery—it took several hours. I cannot remember exactly how many hours, but I remember thinking it was the whole day. Today, this transplant surgery can take anywhere from four to six hours. Waiting was not easy. I remember calling home to our family asking for them to pray. I remember getting several calls asking for updates. I remember my sons being right there with me. Despite the distance, we had a great support system. Strong support is extremely important in these types of situations. We definitely need each other.

It is nearly impossible to keep your mind from drifting down the "what if" lane. What if he does not survive the surgery? What if his body rejects the heart? What if the surgeons make a mistake during the procedure? What if my boys lose their father today? So many negative thoughts can crop up. But as a believer, it is imperative to kill these thoughts before they take root, before we forget the God we serve, the very God of the promise we were standing on. I found it extremely important to rebuke and bind thoughts that did not line up with what God had spoken when we first started on this journey. I had to sit there quietly and battle the enemy who tried to steal the miracle that God was working.

When the surgery was finally over, and they called my name for the family post-surgical update, I was ready. I was ready to be a strength for my husband and our boys. After seeing him and getting an update on what to expect over the next few days, I was ready to move on to the next phase of our journey together. The boys and I headed home to get some rest so we could come back later. We wanted to celebrate with Keith together. To celebrate the removal of Big Blue and to rejoice in the miracle of the new heart.

This was a celebration that was a long time coming. We are so grateful to God that we have received the miracle.

CHAPTER 10

A New Beginning

Delightful anticipation, heading back to the hospital to visit Keith for the first time after the surgery was full of delightful anticipation. We truly did not know what to expect. We had endured a tough six months as a family. We lived at the hospital for six months so to speak. We were now embarking on a new life.

Surprisingly, the recovery was comparable to any other surgery. The staff had him up and walking the next day. Because his recovery was going so well, he was to be discharged about a week later.

My boys and I walked into Keith's room. There was no heartbeat sound in the room—Big Blue was gone. He was sitting up in bed with a huge smile on his face. Still in some pain, but of a whole different kind. We sat and talked for a long while, making plans for his homecoming. It was so exciting. As wonderful as the doctors and nurses were at the Mayo Clinic, we were happy at the thought of leaving them there.

At the same time, it was a little scary. My husband was apprehensive—what if something went wrong once he was at home? Truthfully, I shared this feeling too. Fortunately, the hospital staff was well aware of how traumatic this transition can be. They offered group sessions with other transplant recipients. A safe place where patients and their caregivers could go to discuss feelings and share insight on how they have learned to navigate the process. This type of support was so important to reintroduce Keith back into post-hospital life.

He found a brotherhood of sorts. Spending time with other heart transplant recipients was amazing. We met the family and friends of these fearless people and just talked. Because everyone was at different stages of post-transplant recovery, we were all able to share tips and warnings of things to avoid. These conversations were an invaluable source of encouragement and inspiration.

I will never forget the group session where they all had to sit down and write a letter to the family of their donor. It was a deeply personal letter that took most of them a long time to complete. What do you say to the family of the Person whose gift saved your life? Considering how that same gift was only possible because someone else lost their life? What could you say? How do you say thank you? Needless to say, it was a very emotional session full of gratitude and tears.

I remember bringing my husband's street clothes for the first time in preparation for going home. It was like we were preparing to walk into our future. I remember the big smile on his face as he got dressed. He was so excited about picking up the mantle of father and husband again. The thought of going to our sons' basketball games and swim meets was a source of pure joy for him. It was finally happening—normal life.

Looking back, I understand the importance of this type of support and all the great programs the hospital offered to bring a sense of normal to a tough situation. I would even go as far as saying they were life-saving. I know how the cooking program helped my husband keep his sanity. I thank God for the awesome people who worked with my husband during his stay. Many still keep in touch with him to this day.

Here we are thirteen years later, and Keith is still doing great.

Many of the brotherhood, sadly enough, passed away. Some due to side effects from the medication regimen, some went into rejection, or they just failed to take care of themselves as directed. I can truly say it is of the Lord's goodness that we are still standing today. It is God who has kept his healing hand on my husband.

We have since left Phoenix, the valley of the sun, for the beautiful greenery of North Carolina. Mayo Clinic has transferred his care to a local transplant team, who are also great and extremely competent. Keith is faithful to attend all required checkups and annual procedures. Our sons are now thirty and twenty-six. They have also relocated to North Carolina and are doing very well in their chosen careers.

Keith is now a pastor. We have started our own ministry here, Onward to Perfection Ministries, where we are glad to share God's Word and, of course, Keith's testimony. God has blessed us so much, and it is an honor to share his goodness with the people we meet.

Our journey was hard. It changed us in ways that I cannot fully articulate. But it has also made us better. This journey has brought us closer together, and it has brought us closer to God. I would not have chosen this journey, but I would also not have changed it either. I am profoundly grateful for every lesson learned, for every person God brought into our lives, and thankful to God for preparing us to walk into our purpose.

My prayer for you is that you embrace your journey too so you can also move into your purpose.

Andrea Adams is a wife of thirty-three years and mother of two sons. An ordained Evangelist and teacher of the Gospel. Graduate of University of Phoenix, BS in business management. My great joy in life is to share what God has given to me with his people. My blog: www.onwardtoperfection.com.

I have been a short-term disability claim manager with a major insurance company for fifteen years. I enjoy the opportunity to share our testimony with people who are going through similar situations as encouragement. People need to know success stories that will give them hope at some of their lowest moments. I love to read and watch classic movies on television. I also enjoy spending quality time with my family and friends.

I love to take long walks outdoors for daily exercise.